Galatians

30 Daily Insights from God's Word by **Khan Hui Neon**

Journey Through Galatians
© 2020 by Khan Hui Neon
All rights reserved.

Discovery House is affiliated
with Our Daily Bread Ministries.

Requests for permission to quote
from this book should be directed to:

Permissions Department
Discovery House
P.O. Box 3566
Grand Rapids, MI 49501

Or contact us by email at
permissionsdept@dhp.org

Design by Joshua Tan
Typeset by Grace Goh

978-1-913135-11-9

Printed in the United Kingdom
First Printing in 2020

Foreword

The early church rejoices when the gospel eventually reaches the Gentile world. However, it doesn't take long—about midway through the first century—for the gospel to be challenged by an erroneous teaching that threatens to pervert it. Believers are taught they need to do more than simply trust Jesus in order to be saved: they must also observe the Old Testament law, beginning with circumcision.

New believers in Galatia struggle with this Christ-and-more approach that effectively undermines the sufficiency of Christ's work on the cross and injects human effort into the gospel. This prompts a no-nonsense letter from Paul, who rebukes them for returning to former bondage from which Christ has freed them.

The Galatian controversy shows how easy it is for people to stray. Even today, we often hear of a teaching or belief that insists on a specific rule, conduct, or sacrament—besides faith in Christ—as a requirement for God's acceptance. So, where can we find help to deal with this issue?

The letter to the Galatians will show us the gospel's divine authority, which is the means by which we are saved, and the new life of freedom we enjoy in the Spirit. It challenges us to uphold that freedom and reject any enslavement to human effort. Indeed, the lesson of Galatians is just as relevant today as it was in Paul's time.

May this book strengthen you as you continue to walk with Christ, trusting only in Him.

In Christ Alone,
Khan Hui Neon

We're glad you've decided to join us on a journey into a deeper relationship with Jesus Christ!

For over 50 years, we have been known for our daily Bible reading notes, *Our Daily Bread*. Many readers enjoy the pithy, inspiring, and relevant articles that point them to God and the wisdom and promises of His unchanging Word.

Building on the foundation of *Our Daily Bread*, we have developed this devotional series to help believers spend time with God in His Word, book by book. We trust this daily meditation on God's Word will draw you into a closer relationship with Him through our Lord and Saviour, Jesus Christ.

How to use this resource

READ: This book is designed to be read alongside God's Word as you journey with Him. It offers explanatory notes to help you understand the Scriptures in fresh ways.

REFLECT: The questions are designed to help you respond to God and His Word, letting Him change you from the inside out.

RECORD: The space provided allows you to keep a diary of your journey as you record your thoughts and jot down your responses.

An Overview

Like the letter to the Romans, Galatians highlights two major themes: the first is justification by faith in Christ apart from the law; and the second is that the Spirit is central to living the new life in Christ.

Disturbed by how false teachers are telling Gentile believers that they have to be circumcised to secure their salvation, Paul launches into a stout defence of the doctrine of justification by faith. In this letter, he defends his apostleship and the source of his gospel teaching, as well as the doctrine of justification by faith alone and not works or adherence to the law. He also lays out the practical side of this teaching—what being freed from the law means for our daily living as Christians in the Spirit.

The epistle of Galatians is thus a reminder that we need to have the correct understanding of the gospel and a firm foundation for our faith, because this will affect the way we live and how we relate to God and to other people.

The Structure of Galatians

1:1–10	Salutation and rebuke for believing in a false gospel
1:11–2:21	Defence of Paul's apostleship
3:1–18	Arguments to show salvation by faith alone
3:19–4:7	The law and its purpose
4:8–31	Appeal not to return to bondage
5:1–26	True freedom in Christ
6:1–10	Responsibilities towards others
6:11–18	Final instructions

Key Verse

"Know that a person is not justified by the works of the law, but by faith in Jesus Christ. So we, too, have put our faith in Christ Jesus that we may be justified by faith in Christ and not by the works of the law, because by the works of the law no one will be justified." —Galatians 2:16

Read Galatians 1:1–5

Do you know what the gospel is, how it came about, and how it was transmitted? These are very important questions. If we don't know the answers, we cannot be certain of our salvation and may become vulnerable to all kinds of false teachings. But thanks be to God, for we can find the answers in Paul's letter to the Galatians.

It is worthy to note that Paul begins by emphasising the divine source of his apostleship: he was appointed directly by "Jesus Christ and God the Father" (Galatians 1:1) and therefore, his letter and the gospel it contains carries the full weight of apostolic authority. His recipients are the churches in Galatia (v. 2). While there is some debate as to where Galatia was located (it no longer exists by this name today), most Bible scholars believe that it was a region in southern Asia Minor. Located in modern-day Turkey, this area included Pisidian Antioch, Iconium, Derbe, and Lystra—cities that Paul and Barnabas visited during their first missionary journey (Acts 13:14; 14:1–7). The letter to the Galatians is believed to have been written around AD 48. But what prompted Paul to write?

The churches in Galatia are mostly made up of non-Jewish converts. They became believers after Paul shared the gospel with them during his missionary journey, but they are now being taught a "different gospel" (Galatians 1:6) by false teachers from Jerusalem. These Judaizers—people who follow Jewish religious practices and seek to influence others to do the same (2:14)—are telling them that to be saved, besides believing in Jesus, they also need to be circumcised according to the law of Moses. To Paul, this is a very serious issue, for it goes beyond the question of whether Gentiles need to keep the Jewish law; at stake is the integrity of the gospel as taught by the apostles.

Dispensing with his usual opening greetings, and after a quick introduction and salutation, Paul moves straight on to summarise the gospel in Galatians 1:3–5. He points out the heart of the gospel—that Jesus alone, and not the law, can rescue us from sin and set us right with God.

Paul's succinct introduction lays the groundwork for the rest of the letter, which basically says: hang on to the gospel and its main message of Christ, as preached by God's apostles. Why? Because the gospel is from God, not men. It is God alone who initiates the gospel and who saves us; we are not to add anything to it, nor can we contribute in any way to our own salvation.

What are the dangers of adding to the gospel?

What impact can doing this have on our understanding of God and our salvation?

Read Galatians 1:6–10

Choices and alternatives. These are what people value today. So, the question may be asked: Is there more than one way to be saved? Can we contribute to our salvation?

Paul usually began his letters by praising his readers' faith or diligence, but not in this letter to the Galatians. Instead, right after his introductory remarks (Galatians 1:1–5), he launches into a stinging rebuke of their actions. His rebuke bristles with frustration. In place of the usual thanksgiving we find at the beginning of his other letters, there are strong words of condemnation (vv. 8–9). In verse 6, an astonished Paul asks, "How could you do this? Why are you turning to another gospel?"

Without mincing his words, he declares that anyone who preaches a different gospel—even if he were an angel—deserves nothing less than eternal condemnation (v. 8). There is only one gospel— from God—and it is not negotiable.

Why was Paul so disquieted? It is because of what was happening in the Galatian churches: false teachers were perverting the gospel by teaching that circumcision was necessary for salvation, and the believers were listening to them.

The false teachers, known as Judaizers, were teaching that believers needed to practise certain rituals in order to be recognised as God's people, as required under Mosaic law. But in demanding this, the Judaizers were adding to the gospel, or preaching a "different gospel" (v. 6). In effect, they were saying that God's work in Christ was insufficient, and that man's effort was also needed for salvation. This was such a serious heresy that Paul invokes the worst punishment for the false teachers behind it: "If anybody is preaching to you a gospel other than what you accepted, let them be under God's curse!" (v. 9).

Are Paul's words still relevant today? Perhaps you have been told that trusting in Jesus alone is not enough, and that your salvation needs to be confirmed or supplemented by a specific deed, by adhering to some rules, by undergoing a special experience, or by carrying out some sacramental ritual.

Each of these additions may be good, in and of themselves. But none of them are requirements

When it comes to the gospel, why is it so important to distinguish between what is good and what is essential?

for salvation. To treat them as such would be to undermine the sufficiency of Christ's work on the cross. No matter how helpful they are, or how persuasive or authoritative the people who told you about them are, nothing should be allowed to change the gospel.

The gospel is all about "the grace of Christ" (v. 6). Grace means unearned favour; salvation is something that we cannot do anything to earn. Choices and alternatives? That is pandering to human whims and fancies, at least where the gospel is concerned. Let's follow Paul's example (v. 10) and serve God only by holding to and consistently preaching a law-free gospel.

What could be chipping away at your confidence that the gospel is sufficient for your salvation? What can you learn from today's passage regarding this?

Read Galatians 1:11–12

Today's reading pivots on the question: Is Paul's gospel trustworthy?

The main issue being discussed in Galatians is the integrity of the gospel. Yet, Paul begins with a fairly long section (Galatians 1:11–2:21) in which he spends much time describing how he became an apostle. Why does Paul spend so much time on this?

He does so because the Judaizers are attacking both Paul's apostleship and his teaching. It is likely they are trying to discredit him by sowing suspicion regarding the source of his teaching. Their argument probably goes something like this: Paul is not one of Jesus' original twelve disciples. He was not even a believer when Jesus was around. In fact, he was once a persecutor of the early Christians. So, can his gospel be trusted?

The Judaizers probably reason that if they can convince the Galatians that Paul's apostleship is suspect, then his teaching would not have the same authority as that of the twelve disciples.

That is why Paul goes into detail when sharing his testimony. He has already briefly defended his apostleship in Galatians 1:1, and now he defends his teaching. Paul starts by making it clear that he has received the gospel "by revelation from Jesus Christ" (v. 12), and not from men. In this opening statement, Paul is stressing that his message and authority come directly from God; it is not his own invention. Therefore, the gospel he preaches is trustworthy. God is the source of both his apostleship and teaching.

This truth is important because the authority of the gospel depends on it. We can trust in the gospel of the Bible because God revealed it directly to people He appointed, who then proclaimed it to us; man did not discover or put it together through his own effort. The very basis of our faith and salvation comes from God, and not from any human source.

Today, we have the complete revelation of God's salvation plan recorded for us in the Bible—God's Word—and we can therefore measure any human teaching against it, like the Bereans did when they were taught by Paul. Acts 17:11 records how they "received the message with great eagerness", but also "examined the Scriptures every day to see if what Paul said was true". Not sure if someone is teaching a different gospel? Check it against the Word of God.

What assurances can you draw from the knowledge that the gospel is from God and not from men?

Knowing that the Bible contains God's complete salvation plan for mankind, how can you equip yourself to evaluate a new teaching?

Day 4

Read Galatians 1:13–17

How do we know that the gospel proclaimed by Paul came from God?

After the opening declaration (Galatians 1:11–12), Paul goes on to talk of two things. Firstly, his Damascus Road experience—to show that his conversion and knowledge of the gospel have indeed come directly and personally from Jesus. Given his background as a persecutor of the church (v. 13) and his religious upbringing (v. 14), Paul would never have come to Jesus on his own. Something must have happened. Acts 9 gives a detailed description of how Saul the fearsome persecutor became Paul the passionate missionary.

The once-enemy of the church makes it clear (Galatians 1:15–16) that what drastically turned him around was God's decision to firstly reveal Jesus to him, and then to appoint him to preach Jesus to the Gentiles—God's purpose for Paul from the time of his birth. He did nothing to earn God's call; in fact, he did the very opposite, but God acted out of grace.

Secondly, since his conversion and calling were divinely initiated, Paul did not feel the need to turn to any human authority for verification—including the apostles in Jerusalem.

Instead, he left for Arabia (v. 17) and avoided any human influence (v. 16). He was probably seeking the Holy Spirit's direct guidance to re-examine the same Scriptures that he, a highly trained Pharisee, would have already known so well. But now, with the Holy Spirit's help, his eyes would have been opened to see how all of the Old Testament had in fact been pointing to Jesus as Messiah and that everyone, Jew or Gentile, is saved by faith in Him alone. Being sent personally by Christ to reach out to the Gentiles (v. 16), he needed to make a careful study so that he could explain God's gospel—free of human influence—to people with little or no background knowledge of Scripture.

Paul is confident of the authority of the revelation he received. He is equally confident of his authority as an apostle. Both have divine origin. So, after examining the Scriptures for himself, he returned to Damascus (v. 17), feeling no necessity to check in with the other apostles in Jerusalem before preaching the gospel there.

Paul's teachings are experiential as well as knowledge-based. They are not careless human fabrications, but are founded solidly on Scripture and the direct revelation of God.

Isn't it amazing to discover that here is someone who used to keep the law zealously (v. 14)—and persecuted Christians—but is now preaching grace, not law? Paul is a living demonstration of salvation by grace, not works of the law. It shows God's forgiveness and not His condemnation. And this is the gospel we are sharing!

ThinkThrough

Paul's gospel comes directly from God and is backed up by his transformation from persecutor to missionary. What impact does the gospel have in your life?

How does knowing the gospel's divine origin influence you in sharing it with others?

Read Galatians 1:18–24

No one should preach the gospel on the basis of imitating what others are doing. In this case, imitation is the conduct of a believer without conviction.

Continuing his defence, Paul stresses again the independence of his apostleship and gospel from any man's appointment, wisdom, or teaching.

Following his conversion, Paul did not rush to Jerusalem to seek the counsel of the original twelve disciples. Instead, he waited 3 years before going up to the Holy City to "get acquainted" (Galatians 1:18) with Peter, spending only 15 days with him. It had always been Paul's intention to form and maintain a bond of fellowship with the church in Jerusalem. But even as he visited Peter, he was already ministering as an apostle. Paul highlights that he had limited contact with the other apostles, except for James, Jesus' brother (v. 19). This is to emphasise his apostleship's independence.

To counter the charge that his apostleship and gospel originated from man, Paul invokes the Roman legal praxis: "Before God, I do not lie" (v. 20 NKJV). This is a solemn and legally binding oath. Oath-making was generally discouraged in a Roman court unless it was absolutely necessary. Paul now considers it absolutely necessary for his readers to know that everything he writes to them is true. God is his witness: his is no manmade second-hand gospel; nor Jerusalem-commissioned apostleship.

Without pausing, Paul goes on to recount what happened after his Jerusalem visit. He did not tarry in Judea and spend time there learning the gospel, but immediately set off northward, to the regions of Syria and Cilicia (v. 21). There he remained for some years, having little contact with the Jerusalem church.

This lack of contact extended to all the churches in Judea (v. 22). Clearly, Paul's influence was limited, yet when news of his ministry reached them, they asked, "Haven't you heard how the persecutor who drove many of us out of Jerusalem is now a believer and preaching the gospel? Praise the Lord!" They raised no objection to his gospel, finding it no different from that of the apostles in Jerusalem. Paul writes that though he was "personally unknown" to them (v. 22), yet they "praised God because of me" (v. 24). Being the scattered members of the Jerusalem church, the Judean churches—which had been taught by the apostles—were perhaps the best critics of the authenticity of Paul's apostleship and gospel. Without him seeking it, they gave Paul a resounding affirmation.

Today, our call also comes from God— not man—to share His gospel. Paul was absolutely clear about his calling and the message he proclaimed. Are we as well?

How are you responding to the call by God to preach the gospel (Matthew 28:18–20)?

What are some obstacles that discourage you from sharing the gospel? What can be done to overcome them?

Read Galatians 2:1–5

When we reach out to others with the gospel, we may be tempted to tweak the truth of the gospel to suit different people at different times. But this approach has serious implications.

Paul recounts his second visit to Jerusalem, 14 years after his conversion (Galatians 2:1). This visit took place after a prophet named Agabus predicted a severe famine, prompting the Christians in Antioch to hold a collection to support their brethren in Judea. They sent Paul and Barnabas to deliver the money to fellow believers in Jerusalem (Acts 11:27–30). This time, the two men brought Titus, a Gentile (Greek) believer along (Galatians 2:1).

But Paul had another reason for going. A divine revelation prompted him to present the gospel he was preaching among the Gentiles to those who had become apostles before him. He wanted to ensure he "was not running and had not been running my race in vain" (v. 2). Was he asking the Jerusalem leaders to check whether his teaching was correct, as this verse appears to suggest? Not at all. Paul's real concern was that Christianity could split into two groups—Jewish and Gentile—if Jerusalem did not stand in fellowship with him on the gospel.

To quote from F. F. Bruce, "That would be disastrous; Christ would be divided; and Paul's own work among the Gentiles would be frustrated"[1] because there could end up being one justification for the Jews and another for the Gentiles.

As everyone was Jewish in the Jerusalem church, the circumcision controversy was essentially a Gentile churches' issue. However, with Jerusalem's recognition and support, Paul knew he would not be alone in proclaiming the Christ-only, circumcision-free gospel. There would be no two justifications and God's church would stay united.

What was the Jerusalem leaders' response to Paul's presentation? Titus was not "compelled to be circumcised, even though he was a Greek" (v. 3). To Paul, this was proof enough of their total agreement with his gospel, which was no different from theirs.

Circumcision was an issue in the Gentile churches because false believers had infiltrated their ranks in order to make them slaves to the law (v. 4). But Paul and his co-workers, for the sake of the Gentile believers, refused to compromise, so that Gentile believers could continue to experience the truth of a law-free gospel (v. 5).

What does it mean for us to be united on the gospel?

What can you do to help ensure that there is only one gospel being taught, even when there are different opinions?

We may sometimes wish that the gospel was more appealing to friends and relatives. However, Paul's experience shows that the gospel cannot be tweaked for any reason without serious consequences. There is only one gospel revealed by God and it is based on this gospel that we are saved.

[1] F. F. Bruce, *The Epistle to the Galatians: A Commentary on the Greek Text* (Grand Rapids, MI: Eerdmans Publishing, 1982), 111.

Read Galatians 2:6–10

When it comes to evangelism, can different strategies, target audiences, and workers lead to confusion, disagreement, and disharmony? By studying Paul's teaching, we can avert this possibility.

In Galatians 2:1–5, Paul focused on the Jerusalem leaders' agreement with his gospel. Now he turns his attention to their affirmation of his apostleship and ministry.

Paul mentions "those who were held in high esteem" (v. 6). He is referring to the Jerusalem leaders. As his critics, the Judaizers, have been calling Paul's apostleship into question, Paul emphasises that his apostleship is not inferior to these Jerusalem leaders because "God does not show favouritism" (v. 6). The Judaizers may have been saying, "For your information, two of the leaders who met Paul, Peter (also known as Cephas) and John, were hand-picked by Jesus himself. They lived and trained under Him for 3 years. As for James, why, he was Jesus' own brother! But Paul, who is he?" However, Paul is replying, "I may lack such special connections, but it makes no difference." God does not award apostleship based on who you are related to. Instead, God acts in accordance with His will.

But of greater importance to Paul is that these leaders agreed with his gospel: they added nothing to it (v. 6).

It is interesting to note that instead of focusing on the validity of his apostleship, the Jerusalem leaders discussed mission field demarcation with Paul (vv. 7–9): He was to reach and minister to the Gentiles (uncircumcised) as they were to the Jews (circumcised) (v. 9). Clearly, his apostleship was not an issue with them. The clincher is in verse 8: By working powerfully in Paul just as He had with Peter, God unequivocally authenticated Paul's apostleship; hence, it is not inferior to anyone's.

How did the Jerusalem leaders respond? They gave Paul and Barnabas the right hand of fellowship (v. 9)—symbolising that they recognised what God had done, and accepted that just like them, Paul was already an apostle whose calling was to the Gentiles. That was why they added no condition or demand, except to request that he continue to remember the poor, the very thing that Paul "had been eager to do all along" (v. 10).

Why was there such instant harmony and mutual acceptance among these leaders? It was because they were united in spirit and purpose. They were fully aware that while different people were reaching out to different groups—Peter to the Jews, and Paul to the Gentiles—they shared the same God-given mission, which was to make disciples of all men, and they were preaching the same gospel, of salvation through faith in Christ alone. And that should also be our approach.

How does the phrase "God does not show favouritism" (Galatians 2:6) challenge and encourage you today?

Sometimes it is not easy to accept people whose ministry and calling are different from ours. How do we deal with this situation?

Read Galatians 2:11–14

The gospel is preached not by fine words alone. Consistent behaviour with the truth of the gospel is also required.

Things came to a head when Paul publicly rebuked Peter, whom most Bible scholars agree was the apostle the Judaizers considered the most esteemed. In relating this incident, Paul is giving additional evidence of his apostleship's independence.

Peter had no qualms about eating freely with Gentile believers in the church at Antioch (Galatians 2:11–12), despite the Jews' religious and historical tendency to avoid mixing with the non-circumcised. His presence at the table must have been a great encouragement to the Gentile believers. That is, until more Jews arrived from the Jerusalem church where James was the leader (v. 12). They were probably messengers sent from Jerusalem to Peter.

What was their message? One view is that they had come to warn Peter about the Jewish insurgency happening around that time. Jewish militants would deem anyone socialising with Gentiles and embracing their ways as a traitor. News spread fast. Being one of the Jerusalem church's esteemed pillars (v. 9), Peter's conduct might jeopardise the safety of the church.

If this view is taken, then the "circumcision group" (v. 12) whom Peter was afraid of could have been the militant Jews. There are other views, but at any rate, Peter drew back from fellowship with the Gentiles. The action of this revered apostle had great impact on the other Jewish believers who looked up to him. You can feel Paul's anguish when he writes, "Even Barnabas was led astray" (v. 13)—this happening so soon after their recent visit to Jerusalem (vv. 1–10).

Paul's decisive action in taking a respected leader like Peter to task publicly is noteworthy (v. 14). Many others may not have dared to. Or, they may have felt that it would harm unity among the teachers. How could anyone embarrass an important apostle like Peter? Paul's independence from the other apostles could not have been better expressed.

What did Paul disagree with? At the heart of the issue lay the very basis of the Christian faith. Peter might have acted out of concern for the work and safety of the Jerusalem church, but his action amounted to telling the Gentile Christians, "We cannot have any social interaction with you unless you embrace Jewish practices." Paul might have been worried that the

Gentiles would misconstrue Peter's actions as a call for them to embrace Jewish practices in order to maintain fellowship with Jewish believers. This could lead to the splitting of God's church into two groups and the perversion of the gospel.

We could be equally guilty of Peter's inconsistency and hypocrisy (vv. 13–14) today. We may make what seems to be a small compromise in order to please someone, or to avoid incurring their wrath. But if it affects the integrity of the gospel, we need to ask ourselves: On what basis do we make our decision—on God's eternal truth, or on our fear of man?

Do we compromise the integrity of the gospel in our words, actions, and decisions? What can we do to stop or prevent this from happening?

Paul confronted Peter publicly. Should we do likewise whenever we witness hypocrisy in others?

Read Galatians 2:15–21

Paul turns to the theme that is at the heart of Galatians: We are justified by faith alone, not by works of the law. Justification refers to how we are made right with a holy God. Does this occur when we follow the law or when we place our faith in Jesus? Paul says justification is by faith in Jesus alone. His critics have probably argued that his insistence on justification by faith alone makes him a law-breaker and sinner. To the Jews, anyone living outside of the law is a sinner; hence, Gentiles are deemed as such. And Paul's teaching is leading others to sin, according to his critics.

Here is a possible dramatic dialogue that sums up the argument between Paul and his critics:

"Look," Paul says. "We Jews are a people born and raised under the law, yet we know by experience that justification can't be achieved by keeping it. Why? Because no one can keep it perfectly and therefore, condemnation, not justification, awaits all who try to keep it. That's why we need to look to Christ" (see Galatians 2:15–16).

"Wait a minute," retort the Judaizers. "You are teaching us to abandon the law? Wouldn't that make us lawless sinners (Gentiles), and Christ, the source of your gospel, a promoter of sin?" (see v. 17).

"Absolutely not," Paul shoots back, "for that would contradict everything Christ stands for. However, we would really turn into sinners if we return to the law and fall under its judgment again" (see v. 18).

Paul's point is: If we Jews can't keep the law, why are we demanding that people with no ancestral affiliation keep it?

But how does Paul escape the law's condemnation? He simply dies to it. This will not only free us from having to satisfy its demands, but it will also lead us to live for God (v. 19).

How does Paul die to the law? He puts "I" to death—the old nature that relies on the strict observance of the law for salvation. Bible commentator Eugene A. Nida writes: "To depend on the Law is to put emphasis on one's own powers to do what it requires".[2] Paul crucifies "I" with Christ. Henceforth, he is no longer under its control but under Christ who lives in him (v. 20). Paul knows he can trust Jesus to justify him before God and to help him live for God because Jesus has demonstrated His love for him by dying for him.

In answer to his critics' charge that abandoning the law is sinning against

God, Paul says that far from being condemned, faith in Christ alone results in God's justification. So, why return and submit to the law? That would nullify God's act of grace. If justification by the law is possible, then Christ's death would be pointless (v. 21). No doubt the law is given by God, but Paul has shown that it cannot bring about justification.

Today, we need to ask the same question. What do we depend on for our salvation? Christ or some rule or regulation?

2 D. C. Arichea and E. A. Nida, *A Handbook on Paul's Letter to the Galatians* (New York: United Bible Societies, 1976), 50.

How could observing the Mosaic law turn us into sinners?

We are made righteous by placing our faith in Jesus. Take a moment to praise and thank God for His grace.

Read Galatians 3:1–5

Do you remember how you were saved by God? What convinced you that you were indeed saved?

In today's reading, Paul addresses the Galatian believers pointedly, posing some rhetorical questions to jog their memory. His tone is one of disbelief. They had done so well after turning to Christ, but now they are going backwards. Having understood Paul's proclamation of the gospel and experienced the power of the cross, they are now turning to the law. Clearly, their current behaviour is totally at odds with their initial trust in Christ. How did they abandon their faith in Christ so quickly? "You foolish Galatians!" Paul exclaims in bewilderment, "Who has bewitched you?" (Galatians 3:1).

The Galatians' own spiritual experience is the best proof of the validity of Paul's gospel. He reminds them that the proof of Christ's sufficiency is in the gift of God's Spirit—God's seal of salvation (v. 2). The Spirit's presence in us tells us that we are already justified by Christ. He enables us to lead a life pleasing to God, and guarantees that we will be lifted up with Jesus on the final day. And they had received this wonderful gift by faith, not through observing the law.

Paul is incredulous that the Galatians can be so forgetful and careless. He asks: "Are you so foolish?" (v. 3). We begin the new life by the Spirit's power, but we can't live it to the end by our own strength (of law-observing). Our new life as believers must be lived in its entirety by the power of the Spirit. But for this to come about, we must remain as people of faith.

It is important to note that Paul is not advocating the breaking of rules. As a Jew brought up in the strictest of traditions, he followed Jewish law properly, keeping the Sabbath and observing the various festivals and rites. What he opposed was legalism—keeping the law to be saved.

Finally, Paul reminds the Galatians of some specific experiences they had encountered—probably some unmistakable events that confirmed their new birth in Christ (v. 4). He wonders aloud if these had been in vain and not meant a thing to them.

This goes to show how easily we can forget and be led astray. Did our initial encounter with Christ teach us anything? Have we been walking under the Spirit's power since the moment of conversion? May we never forget how our new life started and how it should be lived to the end—by faith in Christ through the power of the Spirit.

Why do we often forget how we first obtained salvation by faith in Christ? What is the underlying reason?

In our spiritual journey, why can't we supplement the Holy Spirit's power by adding human effort?

Day 11

Read Galatians 3:6–9

Do you have that gnawing feeling that faith in Jesus alone might not be enough to save you? Do you feel the need to contribute to your own salvation? If that describes your situation, then let Paul assure you through Scripture that justification by faith has always been God's chosen way of saving you. Paul bases his argument on what Scripture has revealed.

Paul's opponents taught otherwise. They taught from the Old Testament, so from here on, Paul goes on the offensive and takes the battle to his critics. He quotes the Old Testament extensively to counter the Judaizers' argument, and to show that even in the Old Testament, justification came through faith, not through observance of the law.

For most if not all Jews, Abraham is the most important figure in their rich history, as God selected him to father the race that later became the nation of Israel. Paul's opponents probably pointed out that Abraham had been circumcised to mark him as God's chosen. Perhaps they even taught that only those who observe the circumcision law are Abraham's children.

The Judaizers highly regard Moses, through whom the law came, but

Paul points out in Galatians 3:6 that Abraham, the father of the Jewish nation who predated both Moses and the law, was put right by God ("credited . . . as righteousness") through faith, not by keeping the law (see Romans 4:1–3).

In Romans 4:10, Paul notes that Abraham was declared righteous even before he was circumcised; this rite would take place some 14 years later (Genesis 17:23–26). And the Mosaic law came even later (Galatians 3:17). Clearly, God's justification of the Jews' greatest forefather came as a result of faith, not adherence to any law or rite. By going back not to Moses but to Abraham ("So also Abraham" in v. 6, which means "Consider the case of Abraham") Paul is giving the strongest Scriptural evidence for justification by faith.

But what does this mean for the Gentiles who were not descended from Abraham? In verses 7–9, Paul explains how God told Abraham that all nations would be blessed through him. Anyone who believes like Abraham did—including Gentiles—will be blessed; they become his spiritual children. And since Abraham received God's righteousness by faith alone, his spiritual sons, too, will be made righteous the same way (see Romans 4:11–16).

The lesson is pretty clear: How do we know that faith has always been God's way of saving us? Because God said so in the Old Testament.

Even today, Paul's writings still impact us deeply. Have we fallen into the trap of depending on our feelings, performance, or activities to make us feel secure about our salvation? Let us remember that we are the spiritual descendants of Abraham, because like him, we are also justified by faith alone.

What does it mean to live according to God's promises, given to us through His Word, that we will be saved through faith alone?

As believers in Christ, we are spiritual children of Abraham. How does knowing this affect how we live?

Read Galatians 3:10–14

God has seen to everything that is necessary for our salvation. In today's passage, we will discover how He has given us the perfect salvation.

Having shown why faith alone is enough for salvation, Paul now explains why the law cannot save us. To do this, he delves directly into the heart of Jewish legalism, which is the belief that by observing the Mosaic law, you will be justified before God.

Firstly, Paul quotes from Deuteronomy 27:26 (Galatians 3:10), showing the strict demand of the law: it has to be obeyed perfectly and in its entirety. Since no man (especially the Gentiles) can observe the law perfectly, the outcome is always condemnation (curse), not justification (God's blessing).

Secondly, Paul quotes Habakkuk 2:4 (Galatians 3:11): "The righteous will live by faith." Apparently, justification by faith has always been God's way. Hence, in light of what Scripture has clearly said (from both the Law and the Prophets), to depend on the law for justification is impossible.

Next, quoting Leviticus 18:5 (Galatians 3:12), Paul points out that the law does not depend on faith but on one's ability to carry out its requirements. This approach to justification runs counter to Habakkuk 2:4. Clearly, these two approaches—faith and law—are incompatible. Faith is based on trust and confidence in God, while the law looks to human performance ("live by them" in Leviticus 18:5). Therefore, the Judaizers' insistence that one must have both (faith in Christ and receiving circumcision) for God to justify us makes no sense.

But does the faith approach mean God turns a blind eye to sin? How does He justify us? He dealt with our sin through Christ. Quoting from Deuteronomy 21:23 (Galatians 3:13), Paul shows that when Christ died on our behalf, His death on the cross satisfied the punishment as specified by the law: one who is cursed by God will hang on a tree.

By quoting first Deuteronomy 27:26 and then 21:23, Paul is saying everyone deserves to be cursed because no one can keep the law perfectly. However, Christ rescued us from the curse of the law by taking it on himself. As a result, He came under God's condemnation and became a curse for us when He was hung on a tree (cross) by Roman soldiers. So, far from being overlooked, our sins are fully paid for by Christ. He is indeed our Redeemer and that's why faith in Him alone brings about God's justification. God's way is perfect!

All who come to God through faith in Christ (including Gentiles) will receive the same blessing of justification given to Abraham (Galatians 3:14) and by the same token, they will also receive God's Spirit, the ultimate and undeniable proof of salvation. Praise be to the Lord! He provides for us what we cannot do for ourselves—justification before a holy and righteous God.

As far as salvation is concerned, since faith and law are incompatible, why would some people still try to hold on to both?

How can you live differently knowing that your salvation depends solely on Jesus' sacrifice on the cross, and not on anything you do?

Day 13

Read Galatians 3:15–18

We have looked at Paul's argument about how the law and faith are incompatible when it comes to obtaining salvation. Now, he shows us how God's promise to Abraham cannot be changed or annulled by the coming of the Mosaic law.

Paul reveals that the Judaizers' position is based on a misconception or fallacy—that when God gave the law, His promise to Abraham was annulled. Paul uses "an example from everyday life" (Galatians 3:15)— something so simple that anyone could understand—to show how illogical their position is.

"Brothers and sisters", he affectionately addresses his readers, "it is common knowledge that once a covenant or agreement has been ratified (duly established), it remains in force and cannot be terminated or changed by anyone unilaterally, even if that individual is a party to the contract. Now, if this is true of human contracts, how much more true it is of God's covenants!"

Paul is talking specifically about the covenant—consisting mainly of promises—that God made repeatedly to Abraham (v. 16). The words "covenant" and "promise" are used interchangeably here. Referring to Scripture (Genesis 12:7; 13:15; 24:7),

he points out that there are two recipients of God's promise: Abraham and his Seed, who is Christ. We will consider what role Christ the Seed plays in the next reading.

Paul argues that like all covenants, God's promise to Abraham and his Seed, once confirmed and ratified, cannot be changed. It continues to hold true until its fulfilment. Hence, it is illogical to believe that the coming of the law over 400 years later means that God has terminated, altered, replaced, or superseded His promise (Galatians 3:17).

Summing up in verse 18, Paul states that to believe God's inheritance (the blessing that God has promised) is based on the law is inconsistent with Scriptural revelation: God's inheritance was given to Abraham by a covenant. The promise, received by faith alone, has always been God's way of saving His people; since the law plays no part, to make it essential to salvation is nonsensical.

The law leads to condemnation, but God chose to bless us through the promise of salvation, which includes the blessing that God will justify us (our inheritance) through faith.

How does knowing your salvation can never be threatened by any law affect the way you live?

In what way does knowing justification is by faith in Christ alone help you in sharing the gospel with others?

Do you sometimes doubt your salvation in Christ? As you observe the deep fellowship that other Christians have with God, does it lead you to feel like you're not part of God's family? Are you looking for some other means to help you earn God's acceptance? If that describes your situation, then let Paul's words sink deep into your heart. Our salvation is based on God's unchanging promise. He justifies and accepts us on the basis of faith alone.

Read Galatians 3:19–22

If the law cannot replace the promise of salvation, why did God give it to the Jews in the first place? What value does it have? That must have been the question on the Galatians' minds as they read Paul's comparison of the law and faith.

Lest he should be accused of condemning Moses' law, Paul makes it clear that it had a purpose. "It was put in place by God because you were sinful," he tells his readers simply (see Galatians 3:19). The law is a benchmark: it shows us God's absolute standards of holiness. By it, we can now identify wrongdoing as "transgression"—the crossing into forbidden territory. As such, the law is good.

But Paul is equally quick to point out the inadequacy of the law to save (v. 19). Firstly, it is temporary. Its purpose ended with the arrival of Abraham's Seed, Jesus. And because we can't keep the law perfectly on our own, the law also reminds us that we need a Saviour; it actually points to Christ (the Seed). In short, the law cannot replace the promise. Why? Because God did not intend for it to do what the Seed of the promise does: provide the basis for our justification.

Secondly, the law is inferior to the promise. Paul reminds the Galatians

how the law was given—through angels (v. 19; see Hebrews 2:2). A mediator was also needed to help Israel receive it from the angels. All this implies that there were different parties involved, and thus there would be divergent interests. But Paul says God is one, and He seeks to create one people (both Jews and Gentiles) under Him—something the law cannot effect. If anything, the law makes us more aware of our estrangement from the Holy God and from one another.

Does this mean that Moses' law was opposed to Abraham's covenant? "Absolutely not!" cries Paul (Galatians 3:21). It would be if it was intended as a means of salvation. But God had designed the law for a different purpose, and hence it is not in contention with the Abrahamic covenant. Its role is to reveal sin in us—not to supplant the promise.

The true means of salvation is the Seed of the promise, Jesus (see Romans 3:9–18; Galatians 3:22). Scripture has declared that the entire world is imprisoned by sin (v. 22). We can only escape condemnation by trusting Christ, the Seed, whose work on the cross allows God to fulfil His promise to Abraham by justifying all who believe.

The law has a different purpose and is temporary, but the promise of God will save us eternally. We can never thank God enough for His wonderful promise, because it does not depend on human performance. Anyone who believes will be saved.

Can you think of a rule, ritual, or tradition that could easily distract us from holding onto God's promise in Christ?

Most rules are there for a purpose. How far should we go in following them?

Day 15

Read Galatians 3:23–25

Rules are like crutches. They are there to help us, but they are not our master, and we don't make keeping them the goal of our lives. Likewise, the Mosaic law was given by God for a limited role. In today's reading, Paul elaborates further on what the role is.

He uses two examples to explain to the Galatians how the law relates to them and to the promise of God. First, he likens the law to a prison guard or sentry: "We were held in custody under the law, locked up" (Galatians 3:23). Prior to Christ's coming, like a guard, the law supervised us and restricted our behaviour. It laid out clearly God's standard of perfection and holiness. It also listed the punishments for disobedience, guiding us on how to behave in a manner pleasing to God. Although the law was given to the Jews, Gentiles cannot escape God's condemnation because the entire world is under the bondage of sin (v. 22).

However, the law's role is temporary; "until the faith that was to come would be revealed" (v. 23). What is this "faith" that Paul mentions? It probably refers to the gospel: how Christ enables us to receive the Abrahamic promise through faith in Him (v. 22). Once the gospel arrives—in the person, works, and resurrection

of Christ—the role of the law is over. Jesus has forever freed us from the curse of the law; by faith in Him, we are justified by God. The guard can now be stood down, relieved of his duty, and recalled; his job is over.

Next, Paul uses a term—*paidagogos*—to describe the law (v. 24). The word means guardian, someone who attends to, watches over, and guides a young person in his development. The law is seen as preparing us for and pointing us to the coming of Christ. By revealing our sinfulness as well as our haplessness, the law awakens in us the need for a Saviour, so that "we might be justified by faith" (v. 24).

When Christ arrives, all who believe in Him have come of age (v. 25). The time of development is over. There is no need for either guard or guardian. From now on, all believers ("we", v. 25), Jews or Gentiles, no longer live by the old order, but by faith in the Son of God, who loves us and died for us.

Paul's argument is clear: In the light of this truth, should we still assign a role to the law? No doubt it has a purpose and a limited role, but it cannot impart salvation. Only Jesus Christ can.

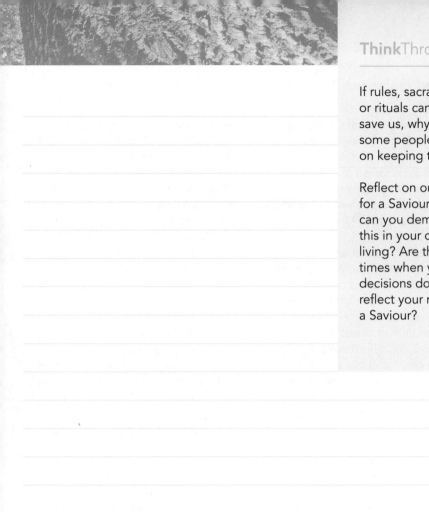

If rules, sacraments, or rituals cannot save us, why do some people insist on keeping them?

Reflect on our need for a Saviour. How can you demonstrate this in your daily living? Are there times when your decisions do not reflect your need for a Saviour?

Day 16

Read Galatians 3:26–29

Paul has shown that with Christ's appearance, believers have come of age, and are no longer under the supervision of rules and regulations. What does this mean, and how does it affect the way we relate to God and other people?

Paul points out that when we (Jews or Gentiles) are saved, we are not only forgiven and acquitted of our sins, but also adopted into the family of God. We become His children through a common faith in Christ Jesus (Galatians 3:26). This means legally there is a change in our status. We become full-grown, mature children of God—unlike a child who needs a guardian, mentor, or nurse. Being freed from the law, we now live in the liberty of Christ.

Paul reminds his readers of the time when they were baptised, publicly committing themselves to Christ and trusting in Him alone for their salvation. It was at that moment they clothed themselves with Christ (v. 27). It is a sign that they have come of age, much like a Roman male child receiving a special garment from his father when he reaches adulthood. They don't live under a guardian—the law—anymore. They have a special garment to prove it: Christ our righteousness.

But that's not all. The Galatians are now "all one in Christ Jesus" (v. 28)— no longer separated by ethnicity, culture, social standing, or gender. All believers are on equal footing in their relationship with God, having the same privilege, status, and value. In Christ, there is one God, one faith, and one people. All former barriers are broken down.

In response to the Judaizers' insistence that Abraham's descendants must keep the law, Paul simply points out that the true offspring of Abraham and heirs to the blessing promised to him are those who exercise faith in Christ (v. 29).

As simple as it sounded, this must have been difficult for the Jews in Paul's day to take in. Their world was divided into Jews and Gentiles. Being Abraham's blood descendants, Jews claimed a special relationship with God that went back hundreds of years. How could Gentiles now claim to be on equal footing with God's chosen people? How could Gentiles, who did not have the law of Moses nor follow it, be their brethren?

Paul's message is clear: We are all of equal value to God because we receive salvation the same way, on the same terms—by faith, and through God's grace alone. There is nothing we can do to obtain righteousness, so there is nothing that can set any of us above another. But just as keeping of the law leads to boasting and accentuates difference, trusting in Christ leads to humility and promotes unity.

What does being adopted into the family of God mean to you? How does it affect your relationship with God and with other people?

Can you identify some possible "barriers" that could lead to division and disunity among believers?

Read Galatians 4:1–7

Do you want to know how you can become an heir to God's promise, and receive the incredible blessings that come with it? If that is your heart's desire, then let Paul take you through the process. He begins by contrasting the present age of spiritual liberty in Christ with the past era of spiritual immaturity under the law. In order to explain, he uses the illustration of a family situation.

The young heir of his parents' estate will own it fully only when he comes of age. Until then, he is a minor and comes under the charge of guardians and trustees (Galatians 4:2). They not only hold the estate in trust, but also act as his tutors, hence subjecting the young heir to control and restrictions. Although he owns the entire estate, the child at this time is no better than a slave (v. 1). When he grows up and comes of age, however, he will be free from supervision, and the estate will be under his full control.

Likewise, we all were once under guardianship. Paul likens this period to slavery under the "elementary principles of the world" (v. 3 ESV). In the case of the Jews, this would have been bondage to their laws and traditions; for Gentiles, perhaps their pagan worship and rites. But that was before Christ came.

This old order ended when God sent His Son at the time He had determined (vv. 2, 4). Christ's coming ushers in an era of spiritual liberty for all who turn to Him. He is the Son of God—the second person in the Trinity—and the Son of Man ("born of a woman", v. 4), and one who though "born under the law" has kept the law perfectly (v. 4). Hence it is He, not the law, who is uniquely placed to save us. The death of this perfect God-Man on the cross for our sins effectively frees us from the bondage of the law, and opens the way for us to "receive adoption to sonship" (v. 5).

God who grants us sonship also makes the "Spirit of his Son" who "calls out 'Abba, Father'" (v. 6) live in our hearts, so that we might be encouraged to approach God as our heavenly Father. The Spirit's presence, therefore, is the evidence that we are God's children. And as God's children, we become God's heirs, possessing all the rights and privileges that this position brings (v. 7). Hence, in the light of this understanding, how could anyone ever want to return to the old order of the law (or pagan worship and rites) and be enslaved again?

What an incredible blessing: from bondage to freedom, and slave to

heir! In Christ, believers have indeed come of age: they are no longer slaves under supervision, but mature children and heirs of God. They live in the liberty of Christ, experiencing the care of God their Father and the power of the indwelling Holy Spirit.

Christ has blessed us incredibly. What does the freedom of Christ mean to you?

How can you respond to this incredible blessing of Christ in concrete terms, this week?

Day 18

Read Galatians 4:8–11

The freedom we enjoy in Christ is very precious. The Son of God secured it for us with His life. We must be careful not to give it up; otherwise we will fall back into slavery.

Addressing the Gentile Galatian believers directly, Paul lays out the threat to their newfound liberty in Christ. The developing crisis triggered by the Judaizers causes Paul to express his fear that somehow he has wasted his efforts on them (Galatians 4:11). This is a serious assertion. Clearly, Paul is not only frustrated but dismayed, because his work would be in vain if the Gentile Galatians exchange one form of slavery for another.

Paul reminds them of their past before conversion, and how they were slaves of false or counterfeit gods (v. 8). But now that they have come to know God through Christ, he cannot understand why they would want to return to these "weak and miserable forces" again (v. 9). In frustration, he rebukes the Galatians: "Do you wish to be enslaved by them all over again?" (v. 9). Better for them to have never experienced salvation and its liberation from bondage than to have obtained and then given it up to return to slavery.

What kind of slavery were the Galatian believers turning to? Paul spells it out plainly in verse 10: "You are observing special days and months and seasons and years!" Listening to the false teachers, they had started to observe the Jewish calendar of festivals, special days, etc. as stipulated by Jewish law, believing that they were essential to salvation.

If they do that, Paul warns, they will be doing something no different from what they did before their conversion: worshipping false gods!

Coming from Paul, a Hebrew of Hebrews, this is quite alarming. How can he equate the keeping of the Jewish sacred calendar to the worshipping of false gods? Is he criticising the very rules and traditions that he was brought up with, and which he continues to observe himself?

Not at all. Paul has unequivocally declared that the law is good (Romans 7:12). He keeps the rules because he is following his cultural heritage, and also because he does not want to stumble other Jews who have become converts. He observes the rules and traditions voluntarily— not because he feels compelled to, and certainly not because they are able to save him or bring him closer to God. But when the observance of the law is made a requirement for salvation, then we would have fallen into slavery under false gods.

God's grace frees us from slavery to sin and the curse of the law. If we start to believe that we must keep a rule or tradition—no matter where it comes from, or how good it is—in order to be saved, then we would have given up the freedom we enjoy in Christ.

Can you identify some "false gods" that can easily distract and enslave us?

What can we do to ensure that we don't give up the freedom we have in Christ?

Read Galatians 4:12–20

Paul's concern for the Galatians never wanes, even in trying times. We can learn much from his example.

Paul's stinging rebuke of the Galatians quickly softens to a personal appeal. They are, after all, his flock. Calling them his brothers and sisters, he begs them, saying: "Be just like me, for I became as you yourselves once were" (see Galatians 4:12). The Galatians are Gentiles who are not subject to the Jewish law (or Jewish legal system) while Paul is a Jew formerly under it. But after his conversion, he dropped the system as a means of salvation and became like them who never had it. "Be like me," Paul says. "Don't adopt what I have given up."

Paul laboured to bring them the gospel so they could be free from bondage to the elementary principles of the world, pagan or Jewish. But he could only do so as someone who was himself totally free in Christ.[3] For this to happen, he had to give up everything (in that nothing has a claim on him except Christ). Having made such personal sacrifice to bring them freedom, it is no wonder he feels he has run in vain if they submit to the law (v. 11).

Paul recalls how well he was treated when they first met: "You did me no wrong," he writes (v. 12). They did not despise him even though he was ill then. Instead, they regarded him as an angel, a messenger from God, and even likened him to Christ Jesus (vv. 13–14). They counted themselves blessed to have heard the gospel from him and even thought nothing of plucking out their eyes for him. To them, it would not have been too great a price to pay in return (v. 15).

So why now the sudden change in attitude, Paul wonders. Is it because he spoke the truth, thus turning himself into their enemy (v. 16)? But isn't being honest with each other what real friends do? Turning to the Judaizers, he asks: Can they be counted as true friends? Unlike him, they were trying to win the Galatians over for a bad reason: they wanted the Galatians' undivided attention by cutting out other teachers and their teachings—particularly Paul—from them (v. 17).

Of course, Paul notes, it is fine to win someone over *as long as the motivation is right*. But this must be true at all times, not just when someone is watching (like when he is present) (v. 18), because the purity, nobility, and moral excellence of our motivation must never be compromised.

This has always been Paul's approach towards the Galatians. When they first met, his sole desire was to share the gospel with them. And now he again labours for their own good—until Christ is formed in them (v. 19)—even if it means he has to suffer like a mother at childbirth. Unlike the Judaizers, his "motherly" heart for them has never changed.

How do we express our concern for others? Look to Paul's fine example. How do we express our concern for others? Like Paul, we should speak the truth to them, but always in love. We should show that our heart is for them and for their good, even if we need to confront them with difficult things.

[3] R. C. H. Lenski, *The Interpretation of St. Paul's Epistles to the Galatians, to the Ephesians and to the Philippians* (Columbus, OH: Lutheran Book Concern, 1937), 217.

Concern for others is never easy. Can you think of some steps to help you follow Paul's example?

Confronting people when they have strayed from the truth can be difficult. Instead of avoiding it, what can we learn from Paul's example on counsel and guidance?

Read Galatians 4:21–31

I s justification by faith a new development in God's salvation plan? In answer to that, Paul argues how Scripture clearly reveals that justification by faith, far from being a new development, has always been God's way of saving mankind. He points to the account of Hagar and Ishmael and of Sarah and Isaac as evidence.

"If you had truly heard and understood the meaning of this story in the Pentateuch (often referred to as Torah or the Law)," Paul says, "How is it possible for any of you to want to be under the law?" (see Galatians 4:21).

Out of Abraham came two sons: Ishmael by Hagar, who was a slave, and Isaac by Sarah, a free woman (v. 22). However, Ishmael was conceived through human effort (flesh) because Sarah thought of giving Abraham an heir through proxy, namely Hagar her handmaid. Isaac, however, was supernaturally conceived, the result of a divine promise, since Sarah had already passed her child-bearing age (v. 23). The sons represent two distinct lineages from Abraham.

But there are implications, Paul continues. The Judaizers claim that they are aligned with Isaac, when in fact they are not. Hagar represents the old covenant based on the law that was enacted at Mount Sinai (v. 24). Why? Because like her, the law—requiring human effort to keep—results in slaves as children, imprisoning all who come under it. Therefore, Paul argues, all who look to the law for salvation, including those presently in Jerusalem, are in bondage (v. 25). They are Hagar's children in the lineage of Ishmael.

However, the Jerusalem that belongs to God is characterised by her free citizens (v. 26), who by faith are set free by Christ from bondage. They are in the lineage of Isaac, the children of the promise and hence the children of Sarah. "And that's who you are," Paul points out to the Galatians (see vv. 28, 31). So why would anyone want to adopt the law and end up aligning with Ishmael?

The right thing to do, Paul notes, is to throw this heretical teaching out, just like God told Abraham to obey Sarah's request to "get rid" of Hagar and Ishmael (v. 30; see Genesis 21:10–12). Salvation will never come through the work of the flesh (as represented by Ishmael). And if it is allowed to stay, Paul warns, it will cause great harm as is happening now (v. 29).

Attacks on our faith happen frequently. The way to overcome them is to hear what God is saying through Scripture: it is through faith in Christ alone that one becomes a free child of Sarah.

In the midst of many voices, why is it important for us to hear what God is saying through Scripture?

How can one belong to the lineage of Isaac and become the child of Sarah?

Read Galatians 5:1–3

Genevan philosopher Jean Jacques Rousseau once said: "To renounce liberty is to renounce being a man." But about 1,600 years before Jean, Paul had already pronounced: to renounce our liberty in Christ is to renounce being Christ's follower. In today's reading, Paul shows us what impact giving up Christ's freedom will have on our personal lives.

Previously, Paul has pointed out that the Galatian believers are already the free children of Sarah. Now, he identifies the source of their freedom: Christ. Galatians 5:1 is considered one of the key verses of Paul's letter to the Galatians; it summarises all he has been saying so far.

Why did Christ set us free? For freedom, Paul asserts. Yes, everything He did on the cross is for the purpose of setting us free. This freedom we have in Christ isn't some imaginary thing or theological fancy. It is real freedom, gained on our behalf by no less than the Son of God, who paid the ultimate price for it. Hence, freedom is the Christian's birthright!

How could we ever give up our birthright? Nations have fought over what they perceive to be theirs, even if it is something transient or temporal. How, then, should we treat our eternal birthright, secured for us by Christ? Stand firm, Paul commands. Never give it up! Tolerate no yoke of any kind, whether pagan or Jewish. In other words, live up to our status in Christ that God has already declared. And don't ever forget, or we will lapse back into slavery.

Putting forward the full weight of his apostolic authority, Paul commands: "Mark my words! I, Paul, tell you . . ." (v. 2). The Galatian controversy is so serious that he feels it necessary to deal with it swiftly and decisively. Without mincing his words, he meets the problem—the call to circumcision—head-on, spelling out the consequence of adopting it (v. 2).

To Paul, it is not so much circumcision per se but what it represents that bothers him; after all, he himself had circumcised Timothy, whose father was Greek (Acts 16:3). But he did it in order to accommodate Jewish sensitivity. The Judaizers, however, believe circumcision is necessary for salvation. This is tantamount to saying that one must first be a Jew before becoming a Christian. And the foolish Galatians are on the verge of adopting it!

Unlike Paul, the Judaizers see circumcision as an initiation rite into Judaism, putting those who accept it under the law (Galatians 5:3),

The consequence of giving up our freedom in Christ is dire. Are we in danger of doing that?

What are some steps you can take to help you stand firm in your freedom and reject any kind of yoke?

thus making observance of the law necessary for salvation. But the consequence is: "Christ will be of no value to you at all" (v. 2). The Galatians would be rejecting all of God's work in Christ and sliding right back into slavery. Christ cannot help them anymore, because He is the only bridge to God's justification; step off it and everything will collapse.

In the light of this warning, no believer should ever give up his birthright in Christ, not in the past nor in the present. No rule, sacrament, or practice should ever be made a necessary component of our salvation.

Read Galatians 5:4–6

Some people think that they can make it to heaven on the basis of their good works. Is this really true? That's the question Paul deals with: How can a sinner be justified before God on judgment day? Can we count on our own efforts, and if not, what can we count on?

Paul has previously stated that it is futile to seek justification through works of the law (Galatians 3:10). Now he adds that it is not only futile, but actually fatal. He issues a stark warning: submission to the law through circumcision will instantly and completely separate us from Christ (5:4). In fact, we will be taking ourselves out of the domain where His grace operates. By adding human effort (law keeping), we no longer solely rely on God's gracious provision in Christ for our salvation; for by submitting to it, we are putting confidence in human effort. As John Calvin observes: "Whoever wants to have a half-Christ loses the whole".[4]

But those of us, Paul continues, who rely solely on faith in Christ can eagerly look forward to that day when God will justify us before everyone (v. 5). We might be justified now through Christ, but the rest of the world neither knows nor acknowledges it. But there will come a day when all who are in Christ shall be revealed and declared righteous by God before the entire universe. No one will be able to dispute the fact or contest the verdict. This hope is kept alive in us always by the power of the indwelling Spirit; it is an assured hope and hence will not put us to shame (Romans 5:5).

In contrast, the law cannot assure us. Those who rely on it (or any human effort) can only "hope" that they will receive a favourable verdict from God on that day. Not so with those who look only to Christ; we already have the Spirit's assurance what the outcome will be.

In God's eyes, Paul tells the Galatians, circumcision (rules, or human effort) really amounts to nothing; the only thing that matters is faith (Galatians 5:6). "For in Christ"—that is, within His sphere of operation—circumcision or un-circumcision is irrelevant (v. 6). It may have been important in the past, but not anymore. So why hang on to it? Paul's message to the Galatians and to us today is: concentrate purely on Christ!

So how can guilty sinners be justified by God on the last day? Through faith in Christ, not by works of the law or human effort. If we look to Christ only, our hope on the last day will be assured.

[4] Charles Partee, *The Theology of John Calvin* (Louisville-London: John Knox Press, 2008), 231.

How does knowing we have an assured hope affect your perspective on life?

Christians can look forward to the day when, before the whole world, God will reveal and declare them righteous. How does that affect your relationship with God?

Read Galatians 5:7–12

The Christian faith is often likened to a marathon. The Galatians started off well when they first heard the gospel, and had every possibility of reaching the goal. But now someone has tripped them, so Paul asks: Who distracted you (Galatians 5:7)? The Judaizers obviously, and they are pushing their agenda. But Paul points out that adopting circumcision is disobeying the truth of the gospel; it is stepping off course, which means instant disqualification. He exhorts them to pull back before it's too late.

The Galatians tripped up perhaps because Paul's opponents are attractive, eloquent, and persuasive speakers, who attempt to sway them to their cause (v. 8). But Paul identifies the source of their persuasion: not God, and thus by implication the devil. Moreover, God calls us to salvation based on the truth He revealed, not some clever human argument, however persuasive it might be.

Paul uses what is probably a proverbial saying to drive home his point (v. 9). The Judaizers are not seeking to overthrow the Galatians' entire belief system. They just want to add a little something more. But when it comes to salvation, even a tiny deviation can result in total ruin, just like the effect of a little yeast in a batch of dough. Paul warns the Galatians: you've already begun observing special occasions (4:10), if you tolerate the Judaizers' insidious heresy further, all will be ruined.

A rumour must be making its rounds which the Judaizers are exploiting in full: that Paul himself sanctions circumcision (5:11). "Remember Timothy?" they might have asked (see Acts 16:3). Not true, Paul retorts. He has preached nothing except the cross—the symbol of God's justification of sinners through faith in His Son, Jesus the Messiah. But the Judaizers find a cursed and dying Messiah, and God's justification without human effort, offensive. "That's why they persecuted me", Paul says. Moreover, he would be agreeing with the Judaizers if the rumour were true. In that case, "the offence of the cross" (Galatians 5:11) would be removed, and salvation through faith in Christ alone would be nullified. What a silly allegation!

Paul reserves his harshest words for his critics. If circumcision is so important, why not go all the way and be castrated like the pagan priests (v. 12)? Is he angry? Perhaps, but it is more than just taking personal offence; at stake here is the truth of the gospel and the preservation of Christ's church.

Paul shows us the importance of tracing the source of all teachings. If they are not from God, we must ignore them, otherwise we can easily be bumped off course.

Why are people so easily won over by "clever" or eloquent persuasions?

What are some ways we can evaluate and trace the source of a teaching?

Read Galatians 5:13–15

Paul has led the Galatians to understand that when they are freed from the bondage of legalism, they have entered into the liberty of Christ. But how do they live out that freedom?

Firstly, Paul states, do not let your freedom be hijacked by the flesh (Galatians 5:13), that old sinful, self-centred nature that is still in you. Know that the flesh always seeks to promote not God's will but itself as the norm of life. The flesh takes pride in human effort. And now that the Galatians are free, it intentionally misleads them into believing that they can do anything they want. If we are not careful, it will use our freedom to satisfy its base desires. That is why it must be stopped from the start, as it perverts the purpose of freedom to which we were called. How, then, should we use our liberty?

In short, we are to "serve one another humbly in love" (v. 13). Paul is not referring to our notion of freedom, but to Christ's perspective on it. Christ liberated us from self-centredness so that we can willingly love others. And we will truly be free when we follow His example of love and serve one another in accordance with God's will. That is how we stop the flesh.

The Old Testament law reflects God's moral obligations for mankind. Paul points out that everything really boils down to just one commandment: love your neighbour as yourself (v. 14). If we carry this out, Paul notes, we would have fulfilled the law, having satisfied its spirit and intention. Therefore, reaching out in love to one another is not only the right use of Christian freedom, but is also the fulfilment of the ultimate moral duty that God places on all who are saved. The children of God seek wholeheartedly to love their neighbour as themselves, and this is what sets them apart.

This commandment must be observed now, Paul demands. It seems that there has been some sharp disagreement among the Galatians, due perhaps to the divisive false teachings. At any rate, it is serious enough for Paul to warn: "Watch out or you will be destroyed by each other" (v. 15). The infighting, if left unchecked, will lead to disunity and a breakdown of fellowship. And that would be disastrous—it would be an abuse of our freedom by the flesh and this conduct is unbecoming of the free children of God.

The liberty of Christ has an immense practical implication: it must be lived out in the way we treat one another—with love.

Name three ways
you can love your
neighbour as
yourself: at work, in
your family, and in
your community.

Christian freedom
is not liberty to act
in any way we want.
It is the freedom
to do God's will,
which is to love
our neighbour as
ourselves. How does
that compare to your
understanding of
freedom?

Read Galatians 5:16–21

The key to living in the liberty of Christ is to deny the flesh by keeping one important commandment: love your neighbour as yourself. This involves two parts. We will look at the first part today, and the second tomorrow.

Paul knows that no external command can coerce us to serve one another humbly in love. The desire must come from within us, created by the Holy Spirit. Paul advises: keep walking in the Spirit (Galatians 5:16); follow Him closely and let Him empower you to do God's will by directing your every thought, word, and deed. Our total immersion in His leading—Paul is quick to promise—will shut out the flesh from our life.

Why is Paul so certain? Because the Spirit absolutely opposes the flesh. He shares nothing in common with it (v. 17). Being its direct opposite, His dominance in our life will spell the end of the flesh. But there is more. While the Spirit can overcome the flesh, the flesh is powerless against the Spirit. Furthermore, Paul continues, the purpose of the Spirit's fight against the flesh is to prevent believers from doing whatever the flesh wants. In short, the Spirit is not only capable, He is willing as well; hence the flesh stands absolutely no chance.

The good news that Paul brings us is that the power of overcoming the flesh lies with the Spirit, not the law—as suggested by the Judaizers—or some other rule, whether Jewish or pagan (v. 18). The flesh loves rules, manipulating them to imprison us. We once could find no way out, but led by the Spirit we are now free to do God's will.

But why is the flesh so detestable? "Just look at how it acts and you will know," Paul replies. He then recites a list comprising five groups of the deeds of the flesh (vv. 19–21): sexual (immorality, impurity, and debauchery); religious (idolatry, witchcraft); relational (hatred, discord, jealousy, fits of rage, selfish ambition, dissensions, factions, and envy); intemperate (drunkenness, orgies); and others. We understand from verse 21 that Paul does not mean the list to be exhaustive ("and the like"). Such acts are so obviously evil that no speculation is needed (v. 19).

Every act has a consequence. God will not sit idly by, and so Paul sternly repeats a warning he must have given out before: those who persist in living this way will neither enjoy nor experience the rule of God in their lives. They will not inherit God's kingdom (v. 21).

By walking in the Spirit, we are free to do God's will. It will also deny the flesh's control over us.

Think of some ways that can help you walk in the Spirit and deny the flesh.

How does understanding the flesh's deeds help you walk in the Spirit?

Read Galatians 5:22–26

Someone once said, "Love is like a rumour. Everyone talks about it, but no one truly knows." Is this true among the children of God? "No," says Paul. We can love one another through the fruit of the Spirit (Galatians 5:22–23).

This fruit comprises the Spirit's manifestations and reflects Christ's character. Whereas "acts" (v. 19), being plural, connote an unbridled, wanton chaos in which the flesh flails in all directions, "fruit" (v. 22)—being singular—reflects the will and character of one Person who follows a clear direction with a single purpose.

Paul lists nine facets of the Spirit's fruit, spread out in three groups.

The first group points to our relationship with God: love, joy, and peace (v. 22). Love refers to God's love (agape). Christians love not in their own way but as God loves them. This leads to joy when we fully realise God's love and grace—justification, freedom, adoption, hope, etc.—and as we experience Him daily through the Spirit's activity. All this culminates in peace: knowing that nothing will ever separate us from God's love in Christ (Romans 8:31–39), we therefore have full confidence in God, believing that He will withhold no blessing from us.

Paul then turns to the believers' relationship with their fellow men. He lists the essential qualities in relating to others: forbearance, kindness, and goodness (Galatians 5:22). Just as God did not give up on us, the Spirit empowers believers to persevere in relating to others. But we don't endure passively with a negative attitude. Instead, we are enabled to respond in kindness, graciously treating others as God treats us. The Spirit also motivates us to do good by being generous to others.

Lastly, Paul shows how the Spirit transforms the way we relate to ourselves. He produces in us faithfulness, gentleness, and self-control (vv. 22–23). Only He can enable us to remain faithful to God and be dependable even under duress; to respond to criticism not with resentment but with gentleness; and to hold in check all our passions and desires.

Such a fruit (of the Spirit)—Paul points out—is beyond the realm of the law. No law can legislate, regulate, or enforce it (v. 23); hence, no amount of law-keeping can produce it.

Looking back, we can see how the acts of the flesh lead to conflict and division while the Spirit's fruit fosters harmony and unity. Furthermore, the Spirit's fruit ultimately enables us to fulfil the greatest commandment: to love God by loving our neighbour as ourselves. What a contrast!

We no longer serve the flesh. In fact, Paul says, when we turn our lives over to Christ Jesus, we have decisively severed our relationship with the flesh (v. 24). "We now live by Christ's Spirit," Paul declares, "so let's fall in line and march under His command!" (see v. 25). Have you heeded Paul's call today?

What are some obstacles that might prevent the Spirit from cultivating His fruit in your life?

How would understanding the fact that you have severed your relationship with the flesh at the point of your conversion affect your life today?

Read Galatians 6:1–5

What does it mean to march under the Spirit's command? Does it mean daily prayer and Bible reading, church attendance on Sunday, or becoming a career Christian worker?

While these are good things in and of themselves, Paul defines it differently. First, he deals with what it is not: self-centredness or pride, leading to provocation and envy (Galatians 5:26). Then, he shows us what it is: support and help for one another in the gentle spirit of Christ (6:1). Selfishness has no place in the liberty of Christ. So, instead of focusing on ourselves, those "who live by the Spirit" must look out for one another, helping each other stay on track (v. 1). To the question, "How do we know we are walking by the Spirit?", the answer is: "You will know because you will have the readiness to help those who have fallen by the wayside (sinned), as Christ would have done."

However, Paul warns, don't let your readiness to help be exploited by the flesh, turning it into an occasion for self-righteousness. Be aware of your own vulnerability to sinning, he says: "Watch yourselves, or you also may be tempted" (v. 1).

Paul next points out a telling characteristic of the community of faith: mutual support (v. 2). This is the blessedness of being Christ's church: no one is left behind to fend for themselves, bearing their burden alone. When we help one another, Paul says, we are fulfilling the law of Christ. But wait a minute, didn't Paul just say that we are freed from the law? The law of Christ, however, is different. It is not about outward observation of rules and regulations, and enforcements with penalties. Rather, it is about helping the brethren, an inner desire created by the Spirit. Hence, as recipients of God's love and care, we have a mutual obligation (law) to care for one another. No believer is exempt.

But what happens if someone refuses to do so, thinking, "I can handle my own burden, and others can handle theirs too"? Is there a necessity for mutual support? Paul says our refusal is an indication that we are deceiving ourselves (v. 3). No one is self-sufficient and we are supportive of others because we understand the need for support for ourselves. So, stop thinking too highly of yourselves.

How, then, should we evaluate ourselves? In verse 4, Paul suggests that we diligently and continually test our own actions. This must be based on God's Word and the Spirit's prompting. The more accurate we are in assessing ourselves, the clearer we are as to our spiritual condition; and if it shows progress, we can take pride in it alone—without comparing ourselves to others—for it is God who made it possible.

Our duty, then, is to see to our own lives and ministry to others (v. 5). Marching under the Spirit's command means fulfilling the law of Christ, which in practical terms means mutual help and support for one another.

How do we help fellow believers bear their burdens in a gentle and loving manner, without downplaying the seriousness of sin or being arrogant ourselves?

Think of some practical steps you can take to express love and support for your fellow Christians.

Day 28

Read Galatians 6:6

Pastors, church leaders, and teachers seem to be always ministering and giving but receiving little in return. Maybe we think them so self-sufficient that it never crosses our mind to return the favour. Paul reminds us that our responsibility to our fellow believers extends to all, including those who teach us.

Just like we have pastors serving in our churches today, elders were appointed to preach, teach, and lead the congregation in the churches of the New Testament (1 Timothy 3:2; 5:17). Paul also reminded the Ephesian elders to "keep watch" over their flock and protect them from false teachings (Acts 20:28–32).

In return, believers are to "share all good things" with their instructors (Galatians 6:6). Traditional teachers of the Jews were paid out of taxes collected from the pupils, but those ministering to the Gentiles had no such salaries.

Paul now extends the same principle from the earlier verses—supporting fellow believers—to teachers as well. It is not just a matter of being practical and generous; there are several compelling reasons why we are to support those who teach us, which Paul lists down in 1 Corinthians 9:5–14.

First, God's law demands it (1 Corinthians 9:9). Paul quotes Deuteronomy 25:4, "Do not muzzle an ox while it is treading out the grain", to show the godly principle of sharing with those who serve us.

Second, Christ commands it: "In the same way, the Lord has commanded that those who preach the gospel should receive their living from the gospel" (1 Corinthians 9:14).

Third, it is a matter of reciprocation. Though he and Barnabas work to support themselves, Paul boldly points out that teachers and preachers should enjoy a portion of the harvest of their labour, just like a farmer and shepherd (v. 7). "If we have sown spiritual seed among you," he asks, "is it too much if we reap a material harvest from you?" (v. 11). This same principle is espoused in Galatians 6:6.

In 1 Timothy 5:17, Paul again notes that "The elders who direct the affairs of the church well are worthy of double honour, especially those whose work is preaching and teaching". So, start expressing your love and support for them today!

Apart from giving to the church, how can we share our good things with those who teach us?

Are we to share only with our "instructors"? Who else in church can we share our good things with today?

Read Galatians 6:7–10

Continuing with the theme of walking by the Spirit—which is fulfilling the law of Christ—Paul now shows us that our motive, attitude, conduct, and actions all have consequences. He uses the analogy of sowing and harvesting to illustrate his point.

He warns that those who persistently defy God, thinking they can get away with it, are deceiving themselves: they will reap what they sow, for God tolerates no wrongdoing (Galatians 6:7). As the harvest is dependent on the seed sown, the input we give in life determines what the consequence will be. Therefore, to expect a different outcome is sheer folly. And like it or not, everyone is involved in sowing here on earth.

Paul then goes on to show there are only two kinds of sowing, leading to two different results. There is no third kind. First, sowing in the flesh will reap destruction (v. 8)—the harvest yields corruption and decay; there will be nothing of value and everything will be destined for destruction. That is the scary part. If we indulge in the flesh, allowing self-centredness to rule over us, the outcome is very clear: destruction. And in this instance, Paul could have in mind Galatians 5:21—of not inheriting the kingdom of God.

Second, in contrast to the flesh, sowing in the Spirit will reap eternal life (v. 8)—a harvest that yields eternal blessedness. This is what walking in the Spirit—or fulfilling the law of Christ—will result in. Paul is not talking about the merits of good works (human efforts) with eternal life as the reward; he is referring to the reward given to those who, *after* being saved by faith in Christ, dedicate their lives in service to God and men ("doing good" in v. 9).

Sowing in the Spirit, however, is hard work. Paul understands, for he himself has experienced much opposition. Hardships, disappointments, and persecutions can conspire to dampen us, but what keeps our spirits up is waiting for the harvest we will reap at the proper time (v. 9). If a farmer can work patiently for an uncertain harvest that lasts temporarily, how much more should believers work for an assured reward of eternal value. Paul urges his readers to hang on, for their harvest is conditioned upon "if we do not give up" (v. 9).

In closing, Paul admonishes his readers—while they still have time on earth, sow in the Spirit, do good to all men, and specifically, to members of the Lord's family (v. 10).

Indeed, God is not mocked; what we do with our lives today will have a direct impact on our harvest at the end times. Start sowing in the Spirit today!

What does it mean for you to do good to all men, and specifically to fellow believers, this week?

Sometimes when we do good, there does not seem to be any visible effect or reward. Think of some ways to deal with the situation when you grow weary of doing good.

Read Galatians 6:11–18

As a Christian, what defines you? How would others describe you as a follower of Christ? What is that one thing that sets you apart from others? Today, as we meditate on Paul's final words to the Galatians, we will learn from him what truly defines a Christian.

"See, I am writing to you in large letters because I want you to know how vital this issue is," Paul begins this section (see Galatians 6:11). Paul has always desired for Christ to be formed in the Galatian believers, and this is an internal work of the Holy Spirit (4:19).

The Judaizers, on the other hand, are pushing their own agenda by putting the external mark of circumcision on them. They want to impress people, Paul points out in Galatians 6:12. Why? Because they want "to avoid being persecuted for the cross of Christ" (6:12). Paul could be referring to the Jewish zealots' threat against those teaching justification by faith or a law-free gospel. The Judaizers are trying to compel the Galatians to be circumcised so as to show they are zealous for the law, thus avoiding persecution for the Jerusalem church—to which they belong—and her daughter churches in Judea.

"They are only interested in boasting how many converts they have won over. It's not like they really want to keep the law," Paul reminds his readers (see v. 13). However, they can boast for all they want over external things. As for him, he will boast only in the cross of Jesus Christ (v. 14). As simple as it sounds, that has immense significance. The cross was a reviled symbol in Paul's day: an offence to the Jews and foolishness to the Greeks (1 Corinthians 1:23). Yet, Paul unashamedly embraces it and takes pride in it. To him, the cross is the expression of God's grace in saving humanity that leaves no room for human pride.

Paul now sees and evaluates life differently. What was once significant, he now considers garbage, and what was once detestable is now important (Philippians 3:8); he no longer lives according to worldly standards. By embracing the cross, the world is permanently severed (crucified) from him, and he from the world (Galatians 6:14).

To Paul, what matters in the new order of Christ is the new united humanity created by God, comprising both Jews and Gentiles. The old order of law-keeping, of circumcision and of Jews and Gentiles, is over; it no longer has any significance (v. 15). As for him, he is beholden to nobody but Jesus Christ, his Master. The many physical scars he carries due to persecutions he has endured, are Jesus' marks of ownership (v. 17). Henceforth, let no one harp on his gospel, missionary policy, or apostleship any more, for everything that he stands for can be traced back to just one source: Christ!

Is this our position too?

Does Paul's position make sense to you? Explain your answer.

What are some barriers that prevent you from taking this position? Surrender them to the Lord today.

Going Deeper in Your Walk with Christ

Whether you're a new Christian or have been a Christian for a while, it's worth taking a journey through the Bible, book by book, to gain a deeper appreciation of who Jesus is and how we can follow Him.

Let faithful Bible teachers be your tour guides and help you draw closer to Christ as you spend time reading and reflecting on His Word.

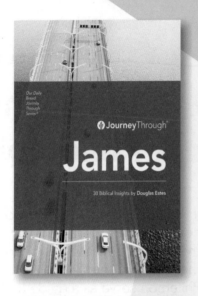

JourneyThrough®

James

30 Biblical Insights by Douglas Estes

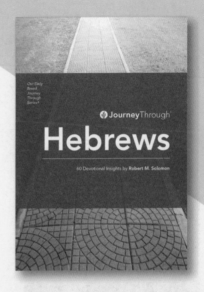

JourneyThrough®

Hebrews

60 Devotional Insights by Robert M. Solomon

JourneyThrough®

Colossians & Philemon

30 Devotional Insights by Mike Raiter

JourneyThrough®

1&2 Timothy

50 Biblical Insights by Robert M. Solomon

Journey Through

Colossians & Philemon

If the Christian life is like a race, how do we ensure that we finish the race, and finish strong? Let the letters to the Colossians and Philemon serve as a guide and source of encouragement as you press on towards this goal. In his letter to the Colossians, the apostle Paul urges the young church to grow strong in Christ and reminds them of His promises, character, and authority. In the letter to Philemon, Paul gives us a wonderful insight into the dynamic, transforming nature of Christian fellowship. Dig into these letters and let the teachings within guide you towards maturity in Christ Jesus.

Mike Raiter is a preacher, preaching trainer, and a former Principal of the Melbourne School of Theology in Australia. He is now the Director of Centre for Biblical Preaching and the author of a number of books, including *Stirrings of the Soul*, which won the 2004 Australian Christian Book of the year award.

For information on our resources, visit **ourdailybread.org**. Alternatively, please contact the office nearest you from the list below, or go to **ourdailybread.org/locations** for the complete list of offices.

BELARUS
Our Daily Bread Ministries
PO Box 82, Minsk, Belarus 220107
belarus@odb.org • (375-17) 2854657; (375-29) 9168799

GERMANY
Our Daily Bread Ministries e.V.
Schulstraße 42, 79540 Lörrach
deutsch@odb.org

IRELAND
Our Daily Bread Ministries
64 Baggot Street Lower, Dublin 2, D02 XC62
ireland@odb.org • +353 (0) 1676 7315

RUSSIA
MISSION Our Daily Bread
PO Box "Our Daily Bread",
str.Vokzalnaya 2, Smolensk, Russia 214961
russia@odb.org • 8(4812)660849; +7(951)7028049

UKRAINE
Christian Mission Our Daily Bread
PO Box 533, Kiev, Ukraine 01004
ukraine@odb.org • +380964407374; +380632112446

UNITED KINGDOM (Europe Regional Office)
Our Daily Bread Ministries
PO Box 1, Millhead, Carnforth, LA5 9ES
europe@odb.org • +44 (0)15395 64149

ourdailybread.org

Sign up to *Journey Through*

We would love to support you with the *Journey Through* series! Please be aware we can only provide one copy of each future *Journey Through* book per reader (previous books from the series are available to purchase).

If you know of other people who would be interested in this series, we can send you introductory *Journey Through* booklets to pass onto them (which include details on how they can easily sign up for the books themselves).

☐ **I would like to regularly receive the *Journey Through* series**

☐ **Please send me ___ copies of the *Journey Through* introductory booklet**

Just complete and return this sign up form to us at:

Our Daily Bread Ministries, PO Box 1, Millhead, Carnforth, LA5 9ES, United Kingdom

Here at Our Daily Bread Ministries we take your privacy seriously. We will only use this personal information to manage your account, and regularly provide you with *Journey Through* series books and offers of other resources, three ministry update letters each year, and occasional additional mailings with news that's relevant to you. We will also send you ministry updates and details of Discovery House products by email if you agree to this. In order to do this we share your details with our UK-based mailing house and Our Daily Bread Ministries in the US. We do not sell or share personal information with anyone for marketing purposes.

Please do not complete and sign this form for anyone but yourself. You do not need to complete this form if you already receive regular copies of *Journey Through* from us.

Full Name (Mr/Mrs/Miss/Ms): _____

Address: _____

_____

Postcode: _____ Tel: _____

Email: _____
☐ I would like to receive email updates and details of Discovery House products.

Signature: _____

All our resources, including *Journey Through*, are available without cost. Many people, making even the smallest of donations, enable Our Daily Bread Ministries to reach others with the life-changing wisdom of the Bible. We are not funded or endowed by any group or denomination.